MEASURES *of* SUCCESS®

for string orchestra

A Comprehensive Musicianship String Method

GAIL V. BARNES • BRIAN BALMAGES • CARRIE LANE GRUSELLE • MICHAEL TROWBRIDGE

Congratulations on choosing to play in the orchestra! Orchestras have played an important role throughout history and have performed for kings, queens, presidents, and countless other historical figures. You are about to begin an exciting musical journey full of rewards and performance opportunities. As you practice, you will find yourself sharing the gift of music with family, friends and audiences. So get ready—your path to success begins now!

ALL-IN-ONE DVD

Your book comes with an All-In-One DVD. It includes tuning notes, instructional videos, and accompaniments for every exercise in the book. You can also put the DVD into your computer to access and transfer the mp3 files to a portable device or burn to a CD. You may also stream or download all videos and recordings by following the instructions on the inside back cover of this book.

HISTORY OF THE VIOLA

The viola is a member of the string family, which also includes the violin, violoncello and double bass. The viola is similar in shape to the violin but is larger. The early ancestors of the violin and viola were the fiddle and the rebec (a European instrument that was derived from an Arabic stringed instrument dating back to the 8th century!). There are stringed instruments all over the world that are used in many cultures. Some of them are plucked while others are also played with the bow.

The viola has a unique voice, similar to the alto voice in a choir. Its range is lower than the violin and higher than the cello.

Many famous composers such as Bach, Beethoven, Dvořák and Haydn played the viola because of its unique sound. Famous viola performers include William Primrose, Yuri Bashmet, Kim Kashkashian and Nokuthula Ngwenyama.

Production: Frank J. Hackinson
Cover Design: Danielle Taylor and Andi Whitmer
Interior Line Drawings: Nina Crittenden, Adrianne Hirosky, Danielle Taylor, and Andi Whitmer

Interior Layout and Design: Andi Whitmer and Ken Mattis
Production Coordinators: Brian Balmages and Ken Mattis
Printer: Tempo Music Press, Inc.

ISBN-13: 978-1-61928-090-8

PARTS OF THE VIOLA AND BOW

PRACTICE GOOD INSTRUMENT CARE!

VIOLA

1. Always handle your instrument with care and avoid extreme temperatures. It can easily be damaged.

2. Your teacher will show you a safe way to remove the instrument from the case and return it.

3. Wipe the instrument clean with a soft cloth.

4. Always remove the shoulder rest before placing the instrument back in the case.

BOW

1. Your teacher will show you how to remove the bow, tighten the bow hair and apply rosin.

2. Always loosen the bow hair before putting the bow away.

SUPPLIES

• rosin
• soft cloth
• shoulder rest
• extra set of strings

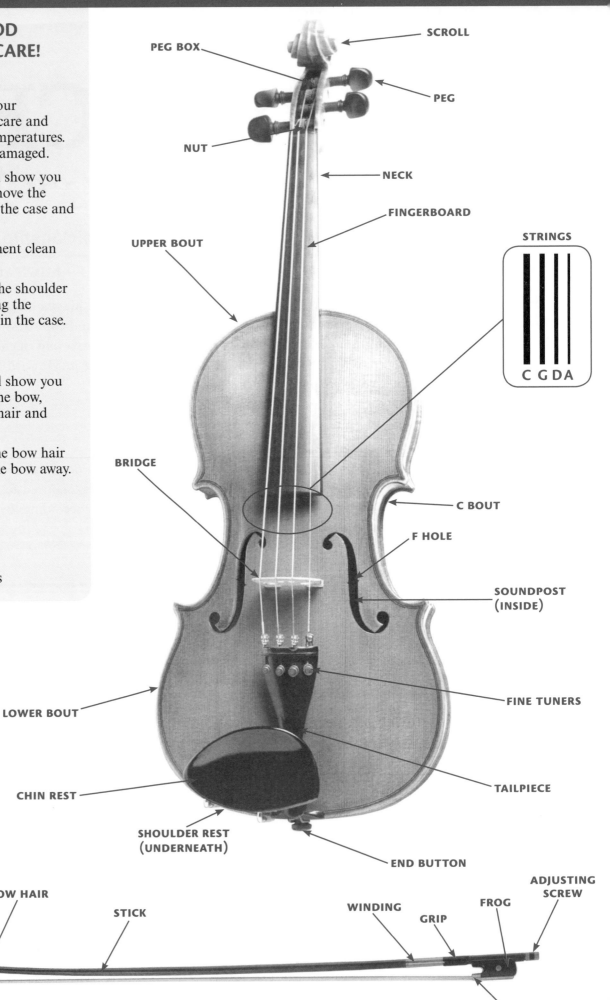

SCROLL
PEG BOX
PEG
NUT
NECK
FINGERBOARD
UPPER BOUT
STRINGS
C G D A
BRIDGE
C BOUT
F HOLE
SOUNDPOST (INSIDE)
FINE TUNERS
LOWER BOUT
TAILPIECE
CHIN REST
SHOULDER REST (UNDERNEATH)
END BUTTON
TIP
BOW HAIR
STICK
WINDING
GRIP
FROG
ADJUSTING SCREW
FERRULE

HOLDING THE INSTRUMENT

Your teacher will determine whether you will start in guitar position or shoulder position. Listen carefully as your teacher explains the proper steps to hold the instrument correctly.

GUITAR POSITION

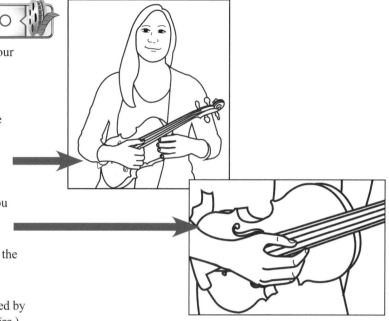

STEP 1 Place your case on the floor on the left side of your chair. Make sure the curved side is facing up. Carefully remove your instrument.

STEP 2 Hold the viola flat against your stomach with the scroll to your left. The neck and scroll should be at an angle similar to the illustration. Check the position of your left hand (on the upper bout).

STEP 3 Move your right thumb over the strings while you place your other fingers under the fingerboard.

STEP 4 Identify the strings. Moving from top to bottom, the open strings are C (lowest pitch), G, D and A.

STEP 5 Pluck each string with your right thumb as instructed by your teacher. Plucking is also called *pizzicato* (*pizz.*).

SHOULDER POSITION

A shoulder rest is essential when holding the instrument in shoulder position. There are many types to choose from, or your teacher may recommend a specific brand.

STEP 1 Place your case on the floor on the left side of your chair. Make sure the curved side is facing up. Carefully remove your instrument.

STEP 2 **Statue of Liberty** - Place your left hand on the upper bout and support the bottom of your viola with the right hand. Hold your instrument directly in front of you with the scroll up.

STEP 3 **Upside down** - Turn your scroll counterclockwise so the scroll is facing down.

STEP 4 **Flat to the ground** - Lift the scroll so the instrument is parallel to the ground at shoulder level.

STEP 5 **Bring it in** - Keeping the instrument parallel to the ground, tuck the instrument under your jaw and on top of your collarbone.

STEP 6 Identify the strings. Moving from your left to right, the open strings are C (lowest pitch), G, D and A.

STEP 7 Pluck each string with your right-hand 1st finger as instructed by your teacher. Plucking is also called *pizzicato* (*pizz.*).

Statue of Liberty

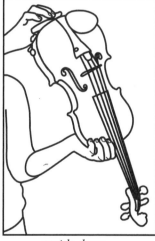
upside down

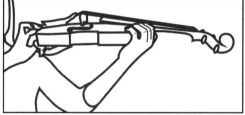
flat to the ground

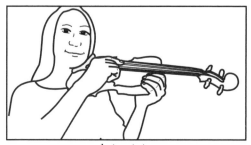
bring it in

SB307VLA

OPUS 1

An **opus** is a number used by composers and publishers who want to organize a group of musical compositions.

BEAT

The **beat** is the pulse of the music. A **rhythm** is a pattern that fits within a steady beat.

1.1 BEAT BOX 1 *While plucking your D string, focus on keeping a steady beat!*

D	D	D	D	(rest!) —	—	—	D	D	D	D	—	—	—	—
1	2	3	4	1	2	3	4	1	2	3	4	1	2	3	4

1.2 BEAT BOX 2 *Practice keeping a steady beat while plucking your A string!*

A	A	A	A	(rest!) —	—	—	A	A	A	A	—	—	—	—
1	2	3	4	1	2	3	4	1	2	3	4	1	2	3	4

1.3 DOUBLE TROUBLE! *Practice playing on your D and A strings!*

D	D	—	A	A	—	A	A	—	D	D	—
1	2	3	1	2	3	1	2	3	1	2	3

MUSIC STAFF
The **music staff** is where notes and rests are written. It has 5 lines and 4 spaces.

measures

BAR LINES
Bar lines divide the music staff into **measures.**

FINAL BAR LINE
A **final bar line** indicates the end of a piece.

NOTES AND RESTS

A **quarter note** is one beat of sound.
A **quarter rest** is one beat of silence.

♩ = 1 beat of sound

𝄽 = 1 beat of silence

1.4 D-LIGHTFUL *Be sure to keep a steady beat, even during the rests!*

pizzicato (pizz.) - pluck the string

1	2	3	4	1	2	3	4	1	2	3	4	1	2	3	4

1.5 DARE TO D *Remember to keep a steady beat for the entire piece!*

pizz.

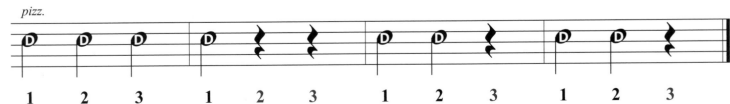

1	2	3	1	2	3	1	2	3	1	2	3

THEORY

ALTO CLEF

An **alto clef** names notes on the staff.
The musical alphabet uses A, B, C, D, E, F, and G.

LINES

F A C E G

SPACES

E G B D F A

TIME SIGNATURE

The top number shows the number of beats in each measure.
The bottom number shows the type of note that receives one beat.

Number of beats in a measure
Type of note that gets one beat

$\frac{4}{4}$ = 4 ♩ $\frac{3}{4}$ = 3 ♩

1.6 A-MAZING

time signature

pizz.

1 2 3 4   1 2 3 4   1 2 3 4   1 2 3 4

1.7 TWO FOR THREE *Notice how the time signature tells you there are three beats in each measure.*

pizz.

1 2 3   1 2 3   1 2 3   1 2 3

THEORY

REPEAT SIGN

A **repeat sign** is a final bar line with two dots.
Without stopping, go back to the beginning
and play the music a second time.

1.8 UPS AND DOWNS

pizz.

repeat sign

1 2 3 4   1 2 3 4   1 2 3 4   1 2 3 4

1.9 COUNT REST-ULA *Count and sing this piece aloud before playing.*

pizz.

SB307VLA

PREPARING THE LEFT HAND

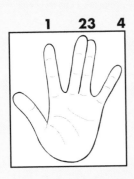

Hold your left hand in front of you, looking at your palm. Space your fingers as shown. Keep this spacing when you move your left hand to the fingerboard.

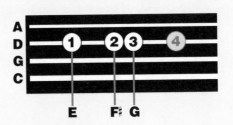

0 – open string
1 – 1st finger
2 – 2nd finger
3 – 3rd finger
4 – 4th finger

NOTES ON THE D STRING

When you move your left hand to the fingerboard, your teacher will help you be sure that:

- Your thumb is opposite your 1st finger
- Your 1st finger and fingerboard form a square
- There is space underneath the neck of the viola between your thumb and first finger

- The tip of your thumb is pointing toward the ceiling
- Your fingers are curved over the string (creating a "tunnel")
- Your wrist is straight and relaxed

G is played with 3 fingers down

F♯ is played with 2 fingers down

E is played with 1 finger down

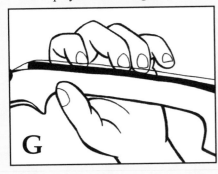

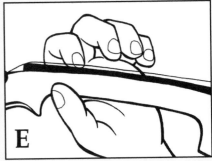

1.10 G WHIZ! *Remember to keep three fingers down when playing G!*

THEORY

ACCIDENTALS: SHARP AND NATURAL

Accidentals are signs that alter a note's pitch. They are placed to the left of the note.
A **sharp** sign raises the pitch of a note by a half-step. It remains raised for the rest of the measure.
A note without an accidental is called **natural.**

1.11 SHARP AS A TACK *Keep both fingers down when playing F♯!*

"F-Sharp"

1.12 TWO STEP MARCH *Keep your fingers over the string, even when they are not being used.*

1.13 MEET E! *Are your 2nd, 3rd, and 4th fingers over the D string?*

NEW NOTE! E

1.14 RUNNING DOWNHILL

1.15 DON'T TELL AUNT RHODY!

American Folk Song

1.16 AU CLAIRE DE LA LUNE *Notice the skip in measure 3. Put down your 1st and 2nd fingers at the same time.*

French Folk Song

1.17 TUNNELING THROUGH *When you see a bracket, keep your fingers down. The A string should tunnel under your fingers. If your A rings clearly while your fingers stay on the D string, you have a clear tunnel!*

HISTORY

MUSIC
Ludwig van Beethoven (1770–1827) was a German composer and pianist. He began to suffer hearing loss at an early age, and by the time his Ninth Symphony and its *Ode to Joy* were performed, he was completely deaf!

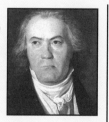

SCIENCE
The same year Beethoven finished his Ninth Symphony, William Buckland wrote the first ever account of fossil bones that had come from a giant reptile. He named it "Megalosaurus" (great lizard), which would later become known as a dinosaur.

WORLD
Also in 1824, Louis Braille had largely completed a new 6-dot system to help the blind and visually impaired read and write. Braille was only 15 years old at the time!

1.18 ODE TO JOY *Keep your fingers down when you see a bracket and strive for a clear tunnel!*

Ludwig van Beethoven

continue to the next line

SB307VLA

8

NOTES ON THE A STRING

LEDGER LINES

Ledger lines extend the staff. Notes written above or below the staff appear with ledger lines.

D is played with 3 fingers down

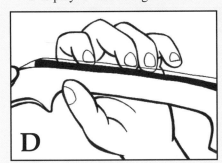

C# is played with 2 fingers down

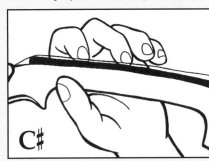

B is played with 1 finger down

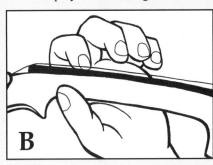

1.19 SAILING THE HIGH Ds *Compare this line to 1.10 G Whiz! Do you notice any similarities?*

1.20 DOWN AND UP

1.21 HIGH OCTANE *Keep your fingers down on the A string when you see a bracket. Listen for a clear, ringing D string!*

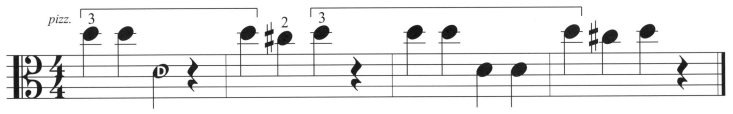

1.22 COLD CROSS BUNS

English Folk Melody

1.23 GROOVIN' GRANDMA

Traditional American Melody

SB307VLA

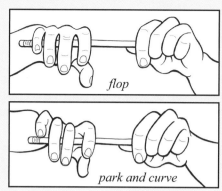

BOW WORKOUT NO. 1: PREPARING THE RIGHT HAND

Using a pencil, do the following:

1 FLOP - Hold the pencil in your left hand, parallel to the floor. **Flop** your right-hand fingers on the pencil.

2 PARK AND CURVE - **Park** the pinky on the pencil. Make sure it is **curved**.

3 SMILE - Place your thumb behind the tallest finger. Your thumb nail should rest against the pencil and the thumb joint is curved like a **smile**.

4 STIR - Rotate your pencil to the right so it is vertical. Check your thumb to be sure it is still curved. Flex fingers and thumb as though you are **stirring** a small cup of soup. Your fingers should be slightly tilted as in the illustration.

1.24 D MAJOR MARCH

1.25 ON THE WAY UP

1.26 MARY HAD A LITTLE LAMB

Traditional

1.27 TRAMPOLINE!

SB307VLA

VIDEO

BOW WORKOUT NO. 2: MOVING FROM THE ELBOW

1 Follow the steps in Bow Workout No. 1 (flop, park and curve, smile, stir).

2 Keep your bow hand relaxed and your thumb curved. Make sure your fingers are tilted slightly.

3 **Point** your left index finger at the crease of your right elbow.

4 **Open and close** the hinge of your elbow. Keep your right shoulder as still and relaxed as possible.

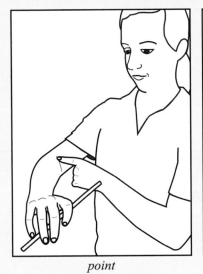
point

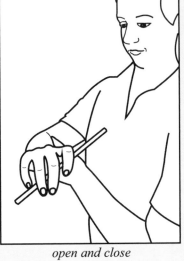
open and close

1.28 BREAKING IT DOWN

THEORY

MAJOR SCALE

A **major scale** has eight notes going up or down in consecutive order. Your D Major Scale includes all the notes you have learned in Opus 1. Notice that the top and bottom notes of the scale are both D.

1.29 D MAJOR SCALE

INTERPRETATION STATION

Listen to the corresponding track on the DVD. Describe the music and how it makes you feel.
Why does it make you feel that way?

SIMON SEZ

Listen to the corresponding track on the DVD. You will hear a series of four-note patterns. Listen to the patterns and
echo them back. *Hint: the first pattern starts on your open D string!*

COMPOSER'S CORNER

A composer is someone who creates original music. It is your turn to be a composer!
Begin by adding the alto clef, time signature, and final barline in the music. Then you
can complete the piece using notes you already know. Guide rhythms have been provided for you.

Add these symbols to your piece!

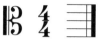

Title: _____ Composer: _____

PENCIL POWER

Review the following notes. Write in each note name below and add the fingering above.

Fingering: ___

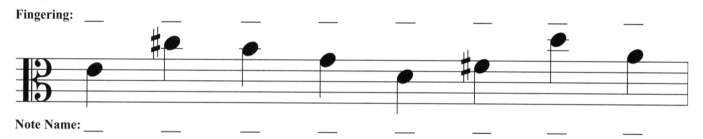

Note Name: ___

CURTAIN UP!

Time to perform! The following music showcases what you have learned in Opus 1.

1.30 STROLLIN' IN THE SAND *Remember to keep your fingers down when possible.*

BOW-NUS!

Demonstrate a great bow hold with a pencil. Open and close your elbow to the following rhythm.

1.31 EL-BOW!

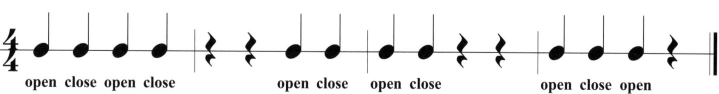

open close open close   open close   open close   open close open

OPUS 2

BOW WORKOUT NO. 3: BOW HOLD

1 Begin by using the early bow hold (your hand will be at the balance point of the bow).

2 Your teacher will show you how much to tighten the bow by turning the adjusting screw clockwise.

3 Hold the bow with both hands making sure the bow hair is facing the floor and the frog of the bow is to your right.

4 While supporting the bow in your left hand, form a good bow hold with your right hand. Remember: *flop, park and curve, smile!*

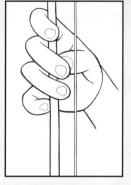

5 Point the tip of the bow in the air with only your right hand. Flex your fingers (*stir!*).

flop, park and curve, smile!

6 Your teacher will determine the ideal time for you to move to a regular bow hold.

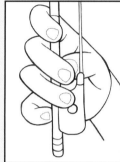

BOW WORKOUT NO. 4: ROSIN BOWING

1 Using your left hand, hold your rosin near your left shoulder with the rosin cake facing away from you.

2 Place the bow on the rosin.

3 Moving from the elbow (like you did when you pointed at the crease), practice moving the bow up and down.

4 Remember to keep your right shoulder as still and relaxed as possible. Open and close from the hinge of your elbow.

 = **down bow**   A down bow symbol looks like the frog of the bow. Lead with the frog and open from the elbow.

V = **up bow**   An up bow symbol looks like the tip of the bow. Lead with the tip and close from the elbow.

2.1 BOW BEAT No. 1 *Rosin bow, making sure you are moving from the elbow, not the shoulder.*

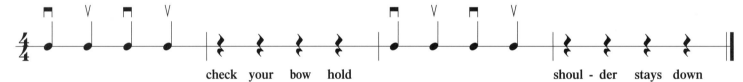

check   your   bow   hold   shoul - der   stays   down

2.2 BOW BEAT No. 2 *Rosin bow. Is your right shoulder still and relaxed while you are bowing?*

1   2   3   1   2   3   1   2   3   1   2   3

FROM ROSIN TO STRING!

1 Place the bow on your D string between the end of the fingerboard and the bridge.

2 Your bow should be parallel to the bridge. Keep your right shoulder down and relaxed.

early bow hold

regular bow hold

2.3 BEST IN BOW *Use an award-winning bow hold and keep the bow parallel to the bridge!*

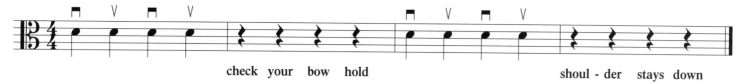

check your bow hold   shoul - der stays down

2.4 ON THE HORIZON *Notice that the time signature tells you there are three beats in each measure.*

1   2   3   1   2   3   1   2   3   1   2   3

2.5 A NEW ANGLE *Make sure you are moving from the elbow, not the shoulder.*

2.6 WALTZ OF THE BOWS

 **ARM LEVELS**

The level of your arm changes when you bow different strings.

Move your **arm down** to play **higher strings.**
Move your **arm up** to play **lower strings.**

2.7 CROSS TRAINING

lower your arm down   raise your arm up

2.8 SWITCH HITTER *Your up bows should sound the same as your down bows!*

(raise!)   (lower!)

2.9 POGO STICK

14

LEFT HAND MEETS RIGHT HAND

You are now ready to combine bowing technique with left-hand fingering!

As you get started, do the following for each exercise:

1. Play *pizzicato*
2. Rosin bow
3. Bow the rhythm on your open D string
4. Put everything together and play as written!

2.10 LEFT BRAIN, RIGHT BRAIN

check your bow hold   shoul - der stays down

2.11 DOWN AND UP

move from el - bow   move from el - bow

2.12 THIRD WHEEL

2.13 THREE FOR THREE *Count and clap before you play.*

2.14 WALKING DOWNSTAIRS

2.15 RUNNING UP AND DOWN

2.16 RUSTIC DANCE

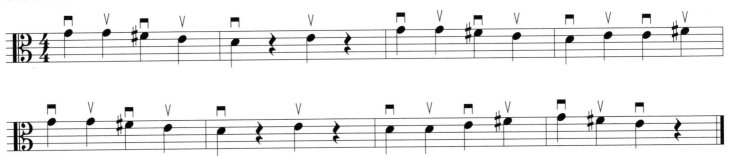

2.17 MOVING UP

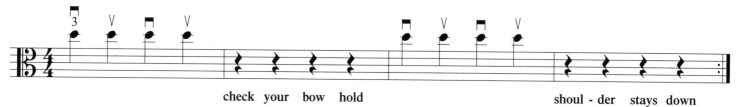

check your bow hold

shoul - der stays down

2.18 DÉJÀ VU

move from el - bow

move from el - bow

2.19 DOWN THE SCALE *Say the fingerings for measures 3 and 4 before you play.*

KEY SIGNATURE

The **key signature** indicates which notes to play sharp or flat. It appears at the beginning of each staff.

Your key signature in 2.20, *D Major General,* tells you that all Fs and Cs should be played as F-sharps and C-sharps. While you already know F♯ and C♯, you will no longer see a sharp sign in front of them.

This is the key of **D Major.**

2.20 D MAJOR GENERAL

key signature

2.21 SCALING THE WALL *When bowings are not marked, continue to alternate down and up bows.*

2.22 RAPPELLING DOWN

16

RETAKE (BOW LIFT)

A **retake (bow lift)** indicates to lift the bow, circle back to the starting position and set the bow back on the string.

2.23 ROCKIN' ROSIN RETAKE *Rosin bow. After playing a down bow, lift the bow, circle back to the frog, and set the bow on the rosin.*

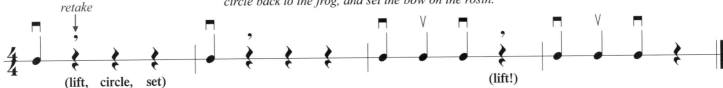

(lift, circle, set)   (lift!)

2.24 RE-TAKE 2 *Play this exercise on your instrument. Remember to execute the same bow motion during the retake - lift, circle, set!*

(lift, circle, set)   (lift!)

2.25 GIVE AND RETAKE

2.26 WALKING HORSES *How many skips are in this piece?*

French Folk Song

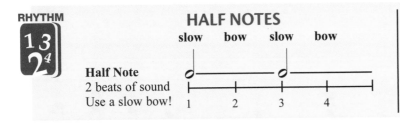

HALF NOTES

slow   bow   slow   bow

Half Note
2 beats of sound
Use a slow bow!

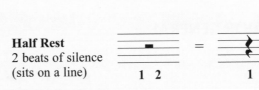

HALF RESTS

Half Rest
2 beats of silence
(sits on a line)

2.27 BOW BEAT *Rosin bow the rhythm. Be sure to keep your shoulders low and open from the elbow. Use a slow bow on half notes!*

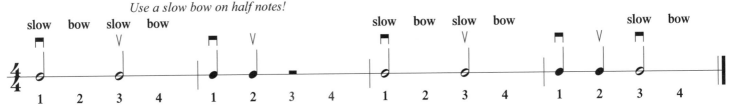

2.28 HALFTIME

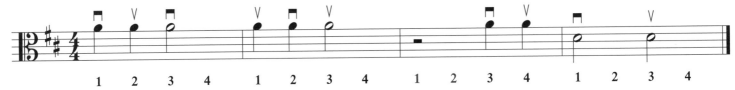

2.29 SLEEPING BABY

French Folk Song

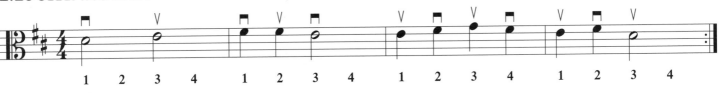

FIRST AND SECOND ENDINGS

At the first ending, play through to the repeat sign. Go back to the beginning or the previous repeat sign and play again. Now skip the first ending – play the second ending instead.

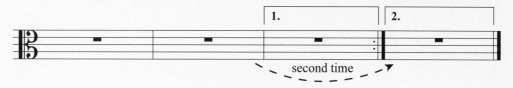

2.30 JINGLE BELLS

James Pierpont

2.31 CIRCUS CLOWN

DUET

A **duet** has two different parts performed simultaneously by two individuals or groups.

2.32 TWO FOR ONE - Duet *Practice playing both parts of this duet.*

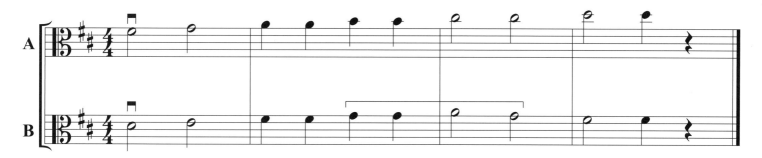

TEMPO MARKINGS

Tempo is the speed of the beat. Music can move at different rates of speed.

Andante - a slow, walking tempo   **Moderato** - a medium tempo   **Allegro** - a fast tempo

2.33 EPIC - Duet

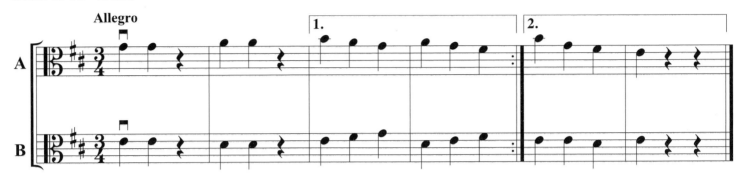

2.34 HOP AROUND
When changing from E to B, your first finger should lift completely off the D string and "hop" over to the A string.

2.35 CHANT
Remember to hop between each E and B in measures 1 and 2!

 HISTORY

MUSIC
Pyotr Ilyich Tchaikovsky (1840–1893) was a Russian composer whose famous works include the *1812 Overture* and *The Nutcracker*. Ironically, *The Nutcracker* was not originally a success, and it was only later that it became one of his most famous compositions.

SCIENCE
In 1893, African-American surgeon Daniel Hale Williams performed one of the first successful open heart surgeries. Later that year, the Johns Hopkins Medical School opened in Baltimore, Maryland.

WORLD
Thomas Edison completed construction of the world's first motion picture studio in West Orange, New Jersey. In Germany, Karl Friedrich Benz received a patent for a gas-powered automobile and eventually founded Mercedes-Benz.

2.36 OVERTURE TO THE NUTCRACKER
Pyotr I. Tchaikovsky

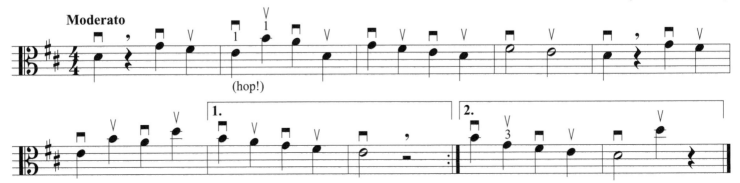

INTERPRETATION STATION

Listen to the corresponding track on the DVD. You will hear two performances of the same piece.
Which one is better and why?

SIMON SEZ

Listen to the corresponding track on the DVD. You will hear a series of four-note patterns. Listen to the patterns and
echo them back. *Hint: the first pattern starts on your open D string!*

COMPOSER'S CORNER

Use the notes and rhythms you have learned to complete the composition. When you are finished, add your own bowings!

Title: _____   Composer: _____

PENCIL POWER

Match the following terms with their definitions.

1. _____ Retake
2. _____ Allegro
3. _____ Andante
4. _____ Duet
5. _____ Arco
6. _____ Pizzicato
7. _____ Moderato
8. _____ Accidental

A. A medium tempo
B. Pluck the string
C. A sign placed to the left of a note that alters its pitch
D. A piece with two different parts performed simultaneously
E. A fast tempo
F. An indication to lift the bow and circle back to the starting position
G. A slow, walking tempo
H. Bow the string

CURTAIN UP!

2.37 TRIFECTA

BOW-NUS!

2.38 WELCOME THE HEROES
There are times when you need to do a retake without a rest present. Work on playing as full a quarter note as possible, then do a small lift / circle before your next down bow.

CURTAIN UP!

ROUND

In a **round**, each musician or group plays the same part, but enters at a different time.

2.39 D MAJOR SCALE - Round *As a group reaches* (2), *the next group should begin playing at* (1).

2.40 LOVE THE SUN - Orchestra Arrangement
(from "Liebst du um Schonheit")

Clara Schumann
arr. Carrie Lane Gruselle

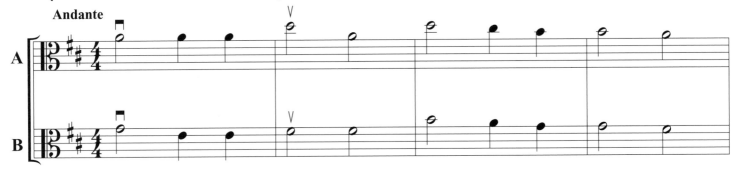

2.41 DEFENDERS OF EARTH - Orchestra Arrangement

Brian Balmages

2.42 ALL THE WOODS ARE WAKING - Round

American Folk Song

2.43 HOLIDAYS UNITED! - Orchestra Arrangement

arr. Brian Balmages

2.44 DOWN ON THE FARM - Orchestra Arrangement

American Folk Song
arr. Carrie Lane Gruselle

OPUS 3

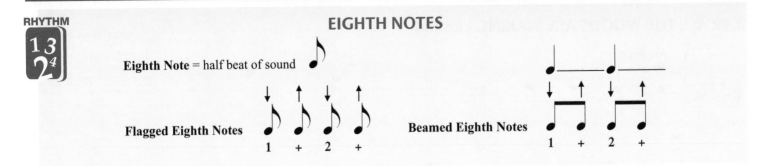

3.1 BOW BEAT

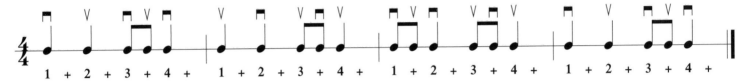

3.2 EIGHTH NOTE CHA-CHA-CHA

3.3 ENTRY OF THE NOBLES *Count and clap this piece before you play.*

BEAM GROUPS

3.4 BOW BEAT

3.5 PIZZA ON THE RIVER!

Pep-pe-ro-ni piz-za   float-ing down the   Mis-sis-sip-pi Ri-ver!   Do you see the   None for me!

RHYTHM 13

TIME SIGNATURE

2/4
2 beats in each measure
Quarter note gets one beat

CONDUCTING IN 2/4 TIME

It is your turn to conduct!
Using your right hand, follow
the diagram to conduct in 2/4 time.

3.6 BOW BEAT *Rosin bow.*

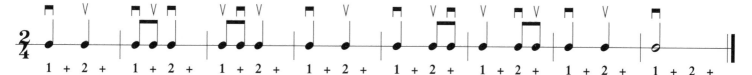

3.7 FIDDLE STICKS

THEME AND VARIATIONS

Composers create a **variation** when they change a melody in some way. While you will hear the differences in each variation, you will still be able to recognize the original theme.

3.8 BOIL THEM CABBAGE DOWN *Bow-nus! Bowing two strings at the same time is called a **double stop**. With your finger tunnels in place, play this exercise while also playing your open A string!*

American Folk Song

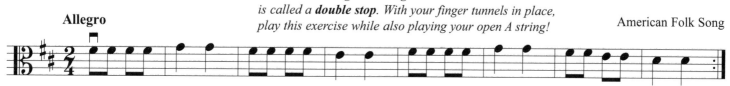

3.9 THREE CABBAGES (Variation 1) *Bow-nus! Play double stops on the D and A strings!*

3.10 CABBAGES GALORE! (Variation 2) *Bow-nus! Play double stops!*

SB307VLA

LEFT-HAND PIZZICATO

+ Play pizzicato with your left-hand 4th finger

Be sure to keep your wrist straight
and your left elbow under the violin.

3.11 4th FINGER MARCH *Make sure you do not collapse the wrist as you play 4th-finger pizzicato.*
Is your left elbow under the violin?

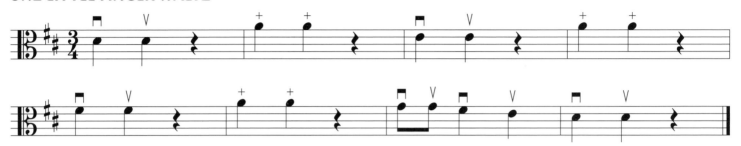

3.12 LITTLE FINGER WALTZ

4th-FINGER A (ON THE D STRING)

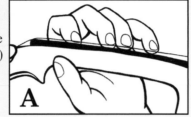

Using 4th-finger A on the D string allows for smoother technique and a richer sound in appropriate places. You can check your intonation (being in tune) by comparing it to your open A. Keep your wrist straight and your left elbow under the viola.

Notice the space between 3rd and 4th fingers!

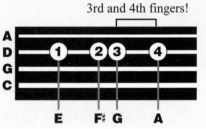

3.13 TWO-WAY A *Keep your fingers down while going to the A string. Is your 4th finger A in tune with your open A?*

3.14 HURON CAROL

French-Canadian Hymn

Andante

COMMON TIME

C The **common time** symbol means the same thing as ⁴⁄₄ time.

CONDUCTING IN ⁴⁄₄ TIME

It is your turn to conduct!
Using your right hand, follow the diagram to conduct in ⁴⁄₄ time.

3.15 FIDDLIN' 4th FINGER

Allegro

THEORY

NOTES ON THE G STRING
(Keep your wrist straight and relaxed)

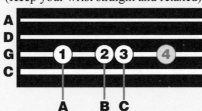

A is played with 1 finger down

B is played with 2 fingers down

C is played with 3 fingers down

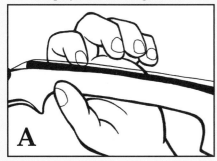

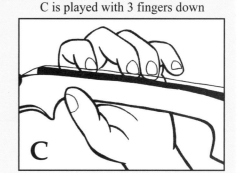

3.16 G FOR ME

NEW NOTE! G

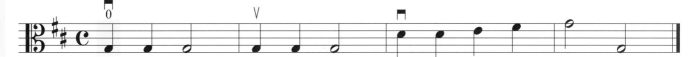

3.17 DARK WATERS *Keep your first finger down where indicated!*

NEW NOTE! A

3.18 FRÉRE JACQUES - Round

French Folk Song

THEORY

D.C. AL FINE

D.C. is an abbreviation for *da capo,* an Italian term that refers to the beginning. At the **D.C. al Fine,** return to the beginning and play again until the **Fine** (the end).

DOUBLE BAR LINE

A **double bar line** indicates the end of one section and the beginning of another.

3.19 FRENCH CAROL

Traditional

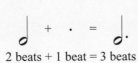 **RHYTHM**

THE RULE OF THE DOT

Adding a dot after a note increases the length of the note by half its value. When adding a dot to a half note, it becomes a **dotted half note**. Use a slower bow (even slower than a half note!).

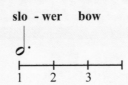

2 beats + 1 beat = 3 beats

CONDUCTING IN 3/4 TIME

Practice conducting in 3/4 time!

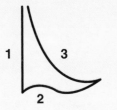

3.20 BOW BEAT *Rosin bow.*

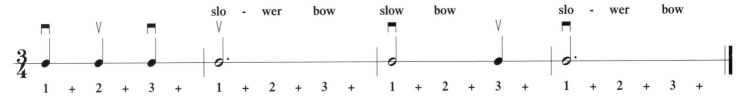

3.21 GETTING A HANDLE ON IT!

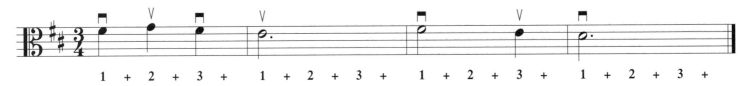

 HISTORY

MUSIC
George F. Handel (1685–1759) was a German-born composer who composed operas, oratorios, orchestral works and more. *Music for the Royal Fireworks* was written when George II of Great Britain hired him to compose music to accompany fireworks in London to commemorate the signing of the Treaty of Aix-la-Chapelle in 1749.

SCIENCE
Sir Isaac Newton, English physicist and mathematician, proposed the laws of motion and universal gravitation. He demonstrated that the motion of objects on Earth and in space could be described by the same principles. He became known as one of the greatest scientists of all time.

WORLD
The Treaty of Aix-la-Chapelle ended the War of the Austrian Succession. The war involved most of the major powers in Europe and centered around the House of Habsburg, whose head was often elected as emperor of the Holy Roman Empire.

3.22 MUSIC FOR THE ROYAL FIREWORKS *Prepare the 1st finger on the G string before you begin.*

George F. Handel

Maestoso (*majestically*)

3.23 TUNING ETUDE *Are all your Gs in tune? How about 4th finger A?*

UPBEATS

Upbeats (pick-up notes) lead into the first full measure of a phrase. When upbeats are used to begin a piece, their combined rhythmic value is often subtracted from the last measure.

3.24 DRY BONES *An upbeat is often played with an up bow!*

Spiritual

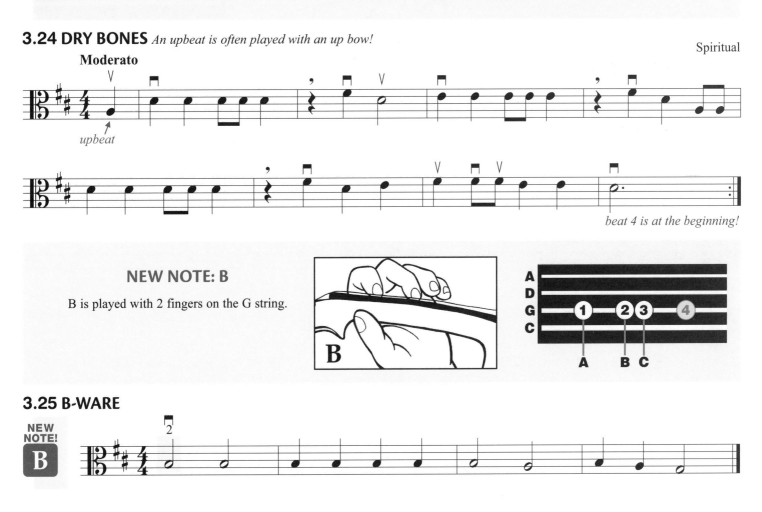

NEW NOTE: B

B is played with 2 fingers on the G string.

3.25 B-WARE

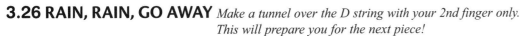

3.26 RAIN, RAIN, GO AWAY *Make a tunnel over the D string with your 2nd finger only. This will prepare you for the next piece!*

Traditional

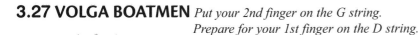

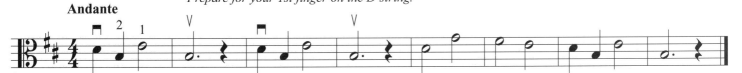

3.27 VOLGA BOATMEN *Put your 2nd finger on the G string. Prepare for your 1st finger on the D string.*

Russian Folk Song

3.28 CHICKEN ON THE FENCE POST

American Folk Song

SB307VLA

NEW NOTE: C

C is played with 3 fingers on the G string.

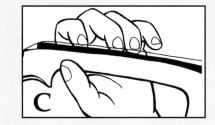

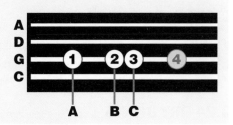

3.29 DOWNS AND UPS

3.30 JUST ABOUT THERE...

NEW KEY SIGNATURE

This is the key of **G Major**.

This key signature indicates that all Fs should be played as F-sharps.

3.31 G MAJOR SCALE

new key signature

3.32 GALOP

Allegro

4th-FINGER D (ON THE G STRING)

Use 4th-finger D for smoother technique and a richer sound in appropriate places.
You can check your intonation by comparing it to your open D.

3.33 LITTLE DUCKLINGS *Intonation check! Are your Ds in measure 2 in tune?*

German Folk Song

Moderato

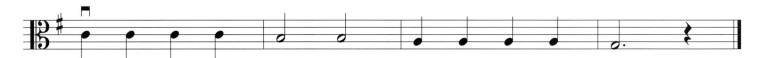

RHYTHM **13 3⁴ 2⁴**

TIE

A **tie** is a curved line that connects notes of the **same pitch.** These notes are bowed together and played to sound like one longer note.

3.34 GIVE IT A TIE

 RHYTHM **13 3⁴ 2⁴**

 VIDEO

SLUR

A **slur** is a curved line that connects notes of **different pitches.** Slurred notes are played **using a single bow**.

3.35 HAPPY SHARK

3.36 SMOOTH WATERS

3.37 THREE TIED MICE

Adaptation

3.38 THREE GLIDING MICE

English Folk Song

3.39 SLURS 'N' SCALES

3.40 A BOW A BEAT

SB307VLA

3.41 ODE TO JOY

Ludwig van Beethoven

HISTORY

MUSIC

Austrian composer **Gustav Mahler** (1860–1911) is best known for his large symphonies. He spent time in New York conducting both the Metropolitan Opera and the New York Philharmonic. Ironically, his first symphony was not well received, and only became popular later.

SCIENCE

Charles Darwin published his theory of evolution and described natural selection as a key mechanism. The Wright Brothers became famous when they built and flew an airplane using a control system they developed to help steer and maintain equilibrium.

WORLD

In Canada, Banff National Park was established and became Canada's first national park. Things in the United States began to cool down when engineer Willis Carrier invented modern air conditioning!

3.42 THEME FROM SYMPHONY No. 1 - Round

Keep your 1st and 2nd fingers down on their respective strings in the last two measures!

Gustav Mahler

keep fingers down!

3.43 CHESTER

William Billings

INTERPRETATION STATION

Listen to the corresponding track on the DVD. You will hear four musical examples, all composed using a different time signature. As you listen, pay close attention to how rhythmic ideas are grouped. Circle the correct time signature for each example.

SIMON SEZ

Listen to the corresponding track on the DVD. You will hear a well-known song. Listen first, sing it, then find the pitches on your instrument. You can then play along with the accompaniment track that follows!

COMPOSER'S CORNER

In this Opus, you learned about theme and variations. Take the following well-known melody and create your own variation.

VARIATION ON TWINKLE, TWINKLE, LITTLE STAR

Name: _____

French Melody

Variation

PENCIL POWER

Solve the following music math problems by notating the correct note value.

CURTAIN UP!

3.44 THE MOREEN *When you see **enclosed repeat signs** (||: :||), repeat the music between the signs (do not go back to the very beginning!).*

Irish Air

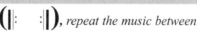

BOW-NUS!

3.45 SERENADE FOR STRINGS *Practice slurring three notes in one bow!*

Pyotr I. Tchaikovsky

CURTAIN UP!

3.46 FANTASTIC FIDDLES - Orchestra Arrangement

Brian Balmages

3.47 DO YOU HEAR? - Round

French Folk Song

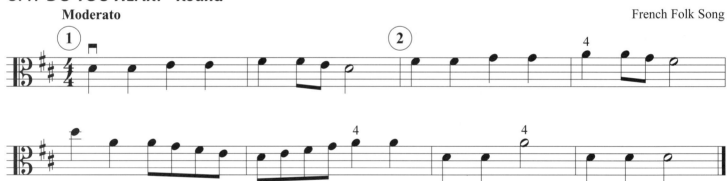

3.48 PRELUDIUM (After J.S. Bach) - Orchestra Arrangement

Brian Balmages

With your bow, stress the first beat of each measure to achieve the proper style.

OPUS 4

STACCATO

Staccato: Play short and separated by stopping the bow between notes.

4.1 SHORT AND SWEET

4.2 DUELING CUCKOOS - Duet

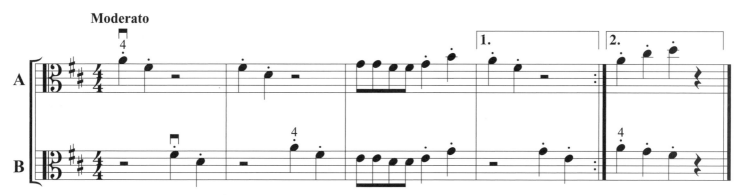

DYNAMICS

Dynamics indicate how loudly or softly to play. Italian terms are often used in music to indicate volume.

p (*piano*) – play softly f (*forte*) – play loudly

4.3 ECHO ETUDE

4.4 SPOOKY GHOSTS AND GOBLINS

SB307VLA

HOOKED BOWING

Play both notes in the same bow direction, stopping the bow between each note.

4.5 HOOK 'EM!

4.6 ALLEGRETTO FROM SYMPHONY No. 7 - Duet

Ludwig van Beethoven

Allegretto (*a tempo between moderato and allegro*)

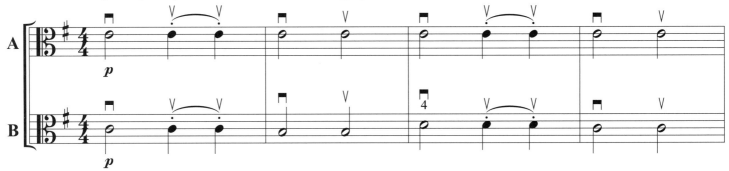

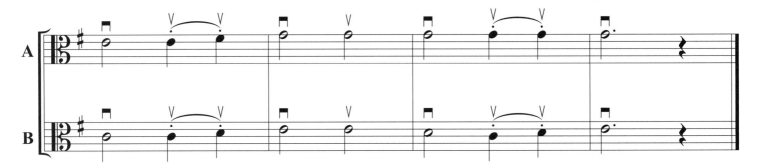

HISTORY

MUSIC
Austrian composer **Wolfgang Amadeus Mozart** (1756–1791) was a child prodigy and composed his first minuet when he was just five years old! In his short 35-year life, he wrote over 600 musical compositions that are still performed today.

SCIENCE
French chemist Antoine Lavoisier recognized and named oxygen. He also wrote the first extensive list of elements and helped develop the metric system. He is widely considered to be the "Father of Modern Chemistry."

WORLD
The thirteen American Colonies issued the *Declaration of Independence,* a statement that justified the American Revolutionary War against Great Britain. The document was approved on July 2nd, but not formally adopted until July 4th, which became Independence Day.

4.7 THEME FROM SONATA No. 11

Wolfgang Amadeus Mozart

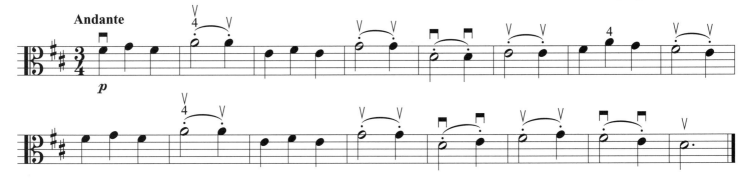

4.8 CRISSCROSS APPLESAUCE

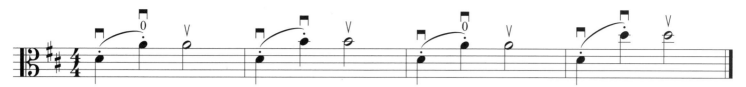

4.9 SMOOTH RIDE

4.10 UP, UP, AWAY

4.11 BOW-DESTRIAN CROSSING

4.12 SEESAW MUSIC

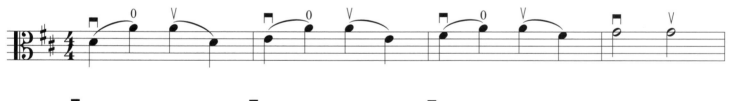

4.13 A LITTLE HERE, A LITTLE THERE *Have your 2nd finger hover over the C# in measure 4.*

4.14 HUSH, LITTLE BABY *Have your 2nd finger hover over the C# in measure 1.*

Traditional

36

LOW 2nd FINGER

Shape your hand as shown in the illustration. Notice that your 1st and 2nd fingers are now touching, and there is space between your 2nd and 3rd fingers. Keep this spacing when you move your hand to the fingerboard.

C NATURAL

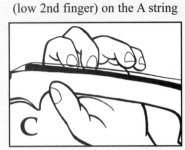

C is played with low 2 (low 2nd finger) on the A string

The fingering for D with a low 2nd finger

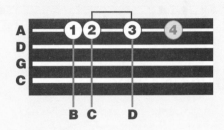

Notice the space between 2nd and 3rd fingers.

ACCIDENTALS

♮ A **natural** sign cancels a sharp or flat. It remains cancelled for the rest of the measure.

(♯) (♮) A **courtesy accidental** reminds you of a sharp, flat, or natural that already applies to a note.

4.15 LOW AND STEADY

NEW NOTE! C

4.16 LOWS AND HIGHS *High 2 (H2) reminds you that C♯ is played with high 2nd finger.*

courtesy accidental

4.17 DANSE HUMORESQUE *Are your octave Ds in tune? Make sure there is space between your 2nd and 3rd fingers.*

4.18 SHAPE SHIFTER *This piece uses two different finger patterns (hand shapes). Isolate each pattern before playing them together.*

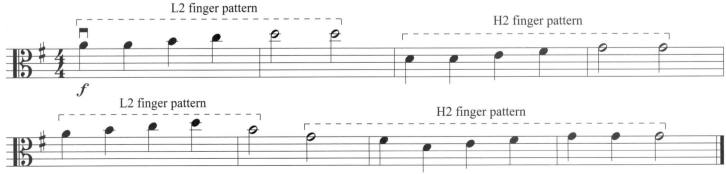

SB307VLA

4.19 DOODLE PRELUDE

4.20 YANKEE DOODLE *Keep 1st and 3rd fingers down where indicated.*

American Folk Song

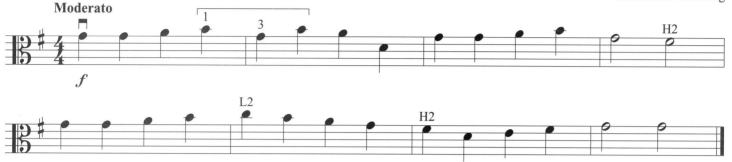

4.21 LA MORISQUE

Tielman Susato

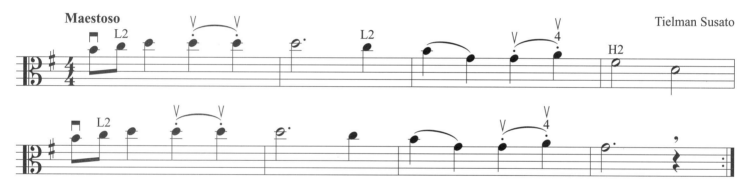

4.22 LOS POLLITOS

Mexican Folk Song

INTERVALS

An **interval** is the distance between two pitches. You can figure out the interval by counting each line and space between notes (include the first and last note). A **half step** is the smallest distance between two pitches. A **whole step** is the combination of two half steps.

4.23 ONE SMALL STEP...

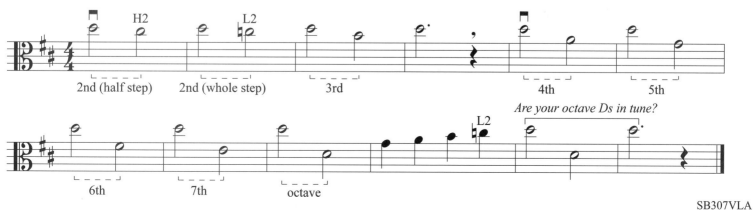

NEW NOTE: F NATURAL

F is played with low 2
(low 2nd finger) on the D string.

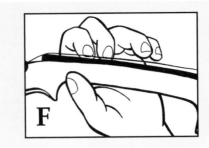

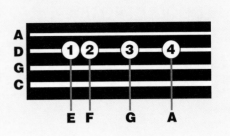

4.24 IT'S ONLY NATURAL

4.25 SNAKE CHANT *This piece has two upbeats.*

4.26 SLIDER *Slide your 2nd finger to move between L2 and H2.*

4.27 LOW-HIGH GALOP

4.28 DIES IRAE

attr. Thomas of Celano

NEW KEY SIGNATURE

This is the key of **C Major**. This key signature indicates all notes are played natural (no sharps or flats).

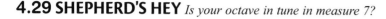

4.29 SHEPHERD'S HEY *Is your octave in tune in measure 7?*

English Folk Song

key signature (no sharps or flats!)

4.30 C MAJOR SCALE

4.31 COUNTRY GARDENS

English Folk Song

4.32 THE MAN ON THE FLYING TRAPEZE *Prepare for the A in measure 3!*

Gaston Lyle

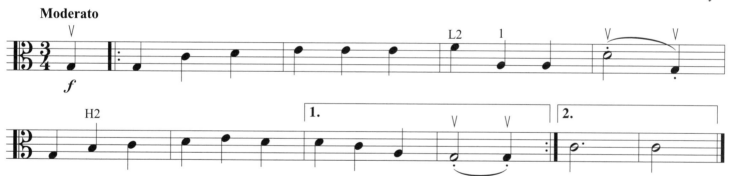

4.33 THEME FROM HANSEL AND GRETEL *For smoother technique, keep 2nd and 3rd fingers down where indicated.*

Engelbert Humperdinck

4.34 FLOWER DRUM SONG

Chinese Folk Song

SB307VLA

40

WHOLE REST

Rest for the entire measure. Always check the time signature!

NOTES ON THE C STRING

D is played with 1 finger down

E is played with low 2nd finger

F is played with 3 fingers down

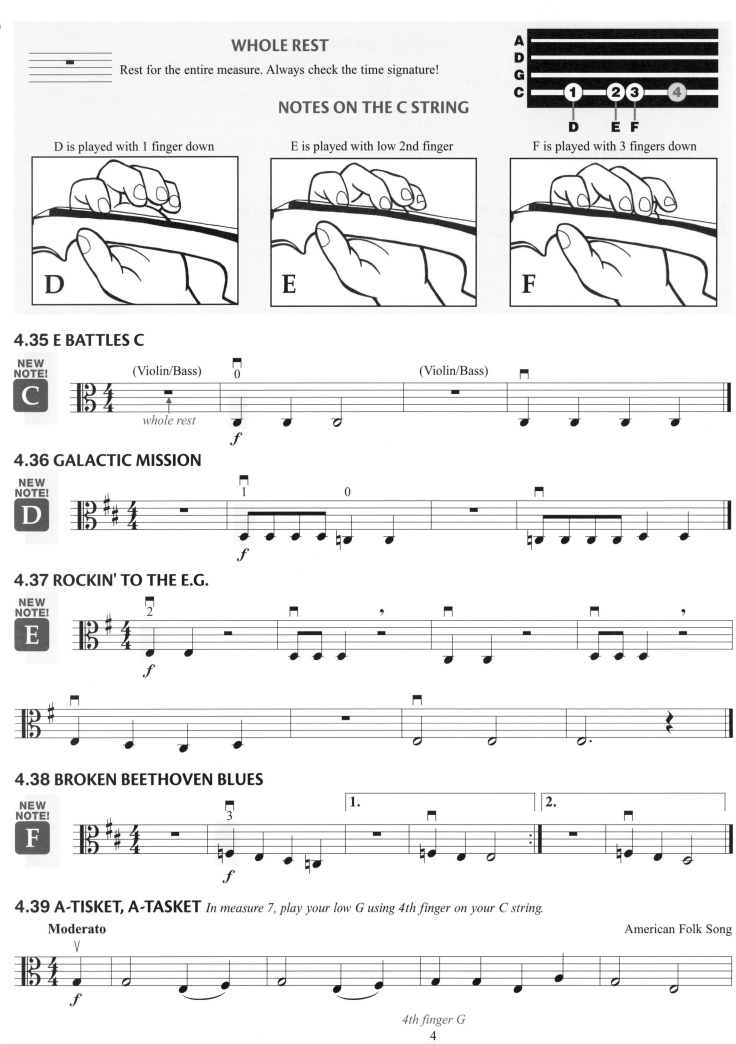

4.35 E BATTLES C

NEW NOTE! C

(Violin/Bass)   (Violin/Bass)

whole rest

4.36 GALACTIC MISSION

NEW NOTE! D

4.37 ROCKIN' TO THE E.G.

NEW NOTE! E

4.38 BROKEN BEETHOVEN BLUES

NEW NOTE! F

1.   2.

4.39 A-TISKET, A-TASKET *In measure 7, play your low G using 4th finger on your C string.*

Moderato   American Folk Song

4th finger G

SB307VLA

41

HISTORY

MUSIC
Franz Schubert (1797–1828) was an Austrian composer who wrote over 600 pieces in his short 32-year lifespan. His *Marche Militaire* was originally written for piano four-hands (2 people playing one piano), but has since been arranged for virtually every type of performing ensemble.

SCIENCE
Louis Agassiz was a Swiss paleontologist who became the first to scientifically suggest the presence of an ice age in Earth's history. He became a leading figure in the study of natural history.

WORLD
A Russian expedition discovered Antarctica in 1820. Years later, Charles Wilkes discovered that it was not just an island, but a whole continent!

NEW NOTE: E

E is played with 4 fingers on the A string.

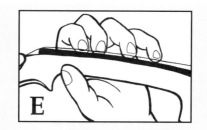
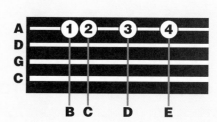

4.40 MARCHE MILITAIRE *In this piece, play your upper E using 4th finger on your A string.*
Franz Schubert

4.41 UP AND AT 'EM!

4.42 TURKISH MARCH

Moderato
Wolfgang Amadeus Mozart

SB307VLA

RHYTHM

WHOLE NOTE

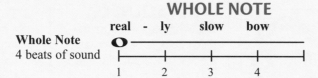

| Whole Note | real - ly slow bow | Use a really slow bow |
| 4 beats of sound | | when playing whole notes! |

4.43 BOW BEAT *Rosin bow.*

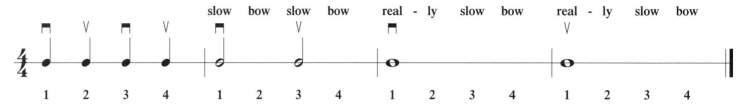

4.44 THE OH-SO-SLOW BOW TO GO

THEORY

DYNAMICS

Crescendo means to gradually play louder.   **Decrescendo** means to gradually play softer.

4.45 CONCERTO THEME

Ludwig van Beethoven

HISTORY

MUSIC

Polish composer **Frédéric Chopin** (1810–1845) was a musical prodigy who began composing at a very early age. He was an accomplished pianist and wrote extensively for the instrument. His *Fantaisie-Impromptu* is one of his best known works, despite the fact he never wanted it to be published!

SCIENCE

In 1842, Christian Doppler, an Austrian physicist, proposed what became known as the Doppler effect. It explained why the pitch of a police siren changed as it approached and passed an observer.

WORLD

In 1836, the Texas Revolution ended when the Republic of Texas was established after a year-long revolution against Mexico. In 1845, it became the 28th state in the U.S.

4.46 FANTAISIE-IMPROMPTU *Notice how the tie connects the E in measure 4 to measure 5, making it last 4 beats.*

Frédéric Chopin

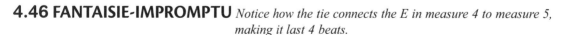

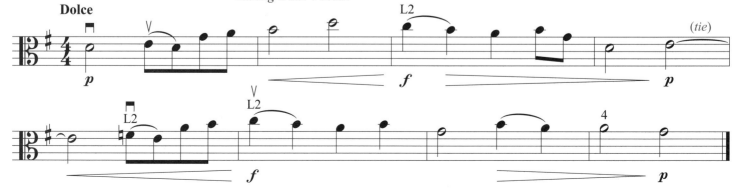

OPUS 4 ENCORE

INTERPRETATION STATION

Listen to the corresponding track on the DVD. For each example, choose the style or tempo marking that best fits the music.

1. Andante   Allegro   3. Maestoso   Misterioso

2. Pesante   Dolce   4. Allegro   Moderato

SIMON SEZ

Listen to the corresponding track on the DVD. You will hear a well-known song. Listen first, sing it, then find the pitches on your instrument. You can then play along with the accompaniment track that follows!

COMPOSER'S CORNER

Improvisation occurs when a performer makes up music on the spot without any previous preparation or written music. Experiment with the guide notes. You can then have a friend or group play the accompaniment line while you improvise (or you can play along with the accompaniment track). *Note: The recording is played 4 times.*

Guide Notes

"ATTITUDE" - Accompaniment Duet

PENCIL POWER

Match the composer with the correct fact by writing in the appropriate letter.

1. _____ Tchaikovsky   5. _____ Beethoven

2. _____ Mahler   6. _____ Handel

3. _____ Schubert   7. _____ Mozart

4. _____ Chopin

A. Continued to compose music after becoming completely deaf
B. Accomplished pianist who also wrote extensively for piano
C. Austrian composer who wrote *Marche Militaire*
D. Child prodigy who composed his first minuet when he was 5 years old
E. German composer who was hired to write music for fireworks in London
F. Composer known for his symphonies who was equally at home as a conductor
G. Russian composer of *The Nutcracker*

CURTAIN UP!

4.47 THE GREAT GATE OF KIEV *Practice playing with a full bow and project a big, beautiful sound!*

Modest Mussorgsky

CURTAIN UP!

4.48 CAN-CAN - Orchestra Arrangement
(from "Orpheus in the Underworld")

Jacques Offenbach
arr. Carrie Lane Gruselle

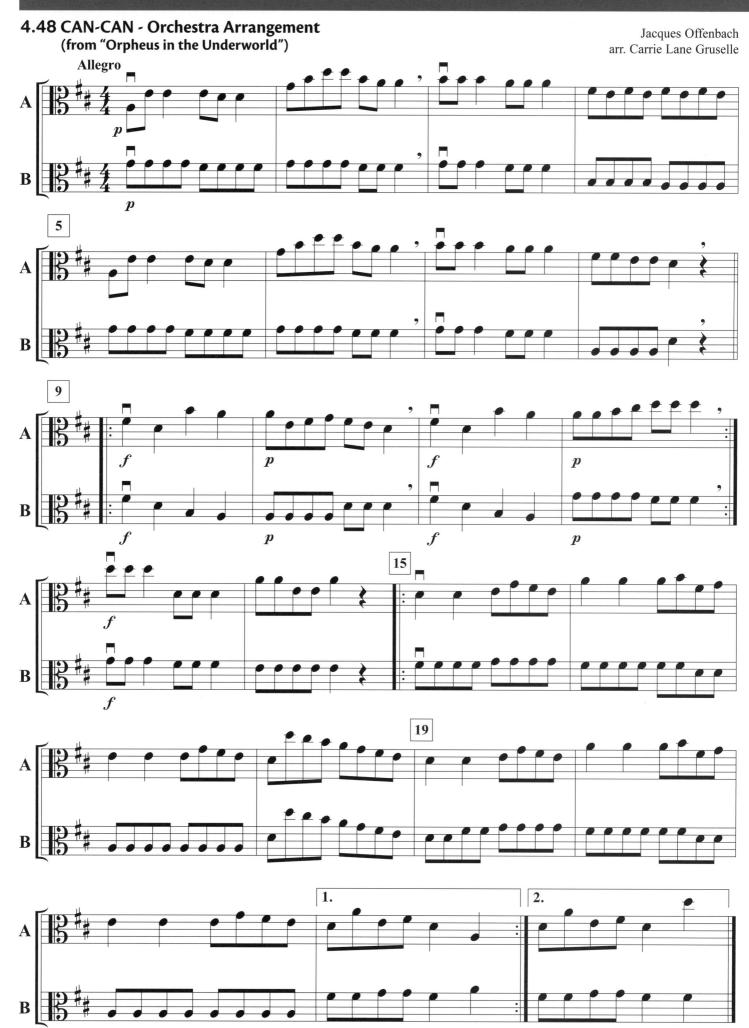

4.49 POWER AND PULSE - Orchestra Arrangement

Brian Balmages

INSTRUMENTAL SOLO

4.50 PETIT RONDO - Solo

Jean-Nicolas Geoffroy
arr. Brian Balmages

Piano Accompaniment

SCALES AND ARPEGGIOS

ARPEGGIO

An **arpeggio** is the first, third, and fifth notes of a major scale played in succession. It may also include the 8th scale note (an octave above the starting note).

Practice each scale using the rhythmic patterns below for each note. Your teacher may suggest additional patterns. Try making up your own!

D MAJOR

Arpeggio

G MAJOR

C MAJOR - Option 1

C MAJOR - Option 2

VIOLA FINGERING CHART

0	L1	1	L2	H2	3	H3/L4	4

STRING								
A	A	A# Bb	B	C	C# Db	D	D# Eb	E
D	D	D# Eb	E	F	F# Gb	G	G# Ab	A
G	G	G# Ab	A	A# Bb	B	C	C# Db	D
C	C	C# Db	D	D# Eb	E	F	F# Gb	G

SB307VLA

INDEX